The Extraordinary World of
BIRDS

Written by
David Lindo

DK | Penguin Random House

Author David Lindo
Illustrator Claire McElfatrick
Senior art editor Claire Patane
Project editor Robin Moul
Designers Polly Appleton, Eleanor Bates, Robert Perry
Editors Jolyon Goddard, Lizzie Munsey
Subject consultant Sacha Barbato
Senior Production controller Francesca Sturiale
Production editor Abi Maxwell
Producer Inderjit Bhullar
Jacket designer Claire Patane
Jacket co-ordinator Isobel Walsh
Picture researcher Rituraj Singh
Senior DTP designer Neeraj Bhatia
Deputy art director Mabel Chan
Managing editor Penny Smith
Publishing director Sarah Larter

First American Edition, 2022
Published in the United States by DK Publishing
1450 Broadway, Suite 801, New York, NY 10018

Copyright © 2022 Dorling Kindersley Limited
DK, a Division of Penguin Random House LLC
22 23 24 25 26 10 9 8 7 6 5 4 3 2 1
001–326080–Mar/2022

A catalog record for this book
is available from the Library of Congress.
ISBN 978-0-7440-5008-0

DK books are available at special discounts when purchased
in bulk for sales promotions, premiums, fund-raising, or
educational use. For details, contact: DK Publishing Special
Markets, 1450 Broadway, Suite 801, New York, NY 10018
SpecialSales@dk.com

Printed and bound in China

For the curious
www.dk.com

This book was made with
Forest Stewardship Council™
certified paper—one small
step in DK's commitment to a
sustainable future.

INTRODUCTION

There is an extraordinary world of birds outside your window. Just take a look!

Come with me to discover why birds are so fascinating. They have features that other animals don't, like feathers, bills, and wings. Most can fly, but the ones that don't have developed super abilities that make them amazing runners or swimmers. Some make incredible sounds or sing beautifully. They can be brightly colored, or secretive and rare. Birds constantly surprise us.

I have loved birds ever since I was a small child, and I hope that you will, too!

David Lindo

CONTENTS

WHAT IS A BIRD?

A bird is an animal that comes in an enormous range of shapes, sizes, and colors. Each type of bird is amazing in its own way.

One of the most fantastic things about birds—**aside from the jaw-dropping fact that they are living dinosaurs**—is how different they are from each other. They all have feathers and wings, but not all of them can fly. They eat many types of food and have bills shaped to suit their diets. Their nests, eggs, and chicks can look very different, too. Birds are truly diverse!

The female firecrest has a **yellow head stripe**, while the male's is a **fiery orange**.

Birds look and behave like their dinosaur ancestors.

Jixiangornis
(124 million
years ago)

Microraptor
(125 million
years ago)

Distant relatives

Birds are part of a dinosaur family called **theropods.** Theropods were often small and fast. They had big brains, sharp senses, and light skeletons. All theropods had feathers, and many had wings.

Confuciusornis
(125 million
years ago)

Tyrannosaurus rex
(68 million
years ago)

Jeholornis
(120 million
years ago)

The first bird

When the first fossilized bird was discovered in 1861, scientists were amazed. This fossil, ***Archaeopteryx,*** had feathers like a bird—but it also had teeth and claws like a dinosaur. People began to realize they were related.

Beishanlong grandis
(120 million
years ago)

Archaeopteryx
(150 million
years ago)

Common city pigeon
Even pigeons
are related
to dinosaurs.

Dinosaurs today
Scientists believe that
dinosaurs were wiped out by
a meteorite hitting the Earth.
But a few theropods survived
this event. Over millions of
years, they evolved until there
were over 10,000 types of
dinosaurs—our birds.

Living dinosaurs

Birds are dinosaurs in the same way that humans are mammals—they are one branch of the dinosaur family tree. Over time they evolved, a tiny bit at a time, slowly becoming the birds we see around us today.

Flying

Although other animals, such as insects and bats, can fly, **birds are the true masters of the air.** Some flutter short distances, while others stay aloft for months—perhaps even years—without ever touching the ground.

Common chaffinch

To be light enough for flight, birds have **hollow yet strong bones.**

Feathers are lightweight and kept in shape by connecting barbs.

BIRD BODIES

Birds are nature's ultimate flying machines. Every element of their bodies serves to keep them airborne.

The tail acts as a rudder, helping a bird **change direction or slow down** in the air.

Birds have aerodynamic bodies that allow them to cut perfectly through the air when flying.

Common eider

The world's heaviest duck can fly as fast as **70 mph (110 kph).**

Built for a life in the sky, **swifts are streamlined to perfection.**

African palm swift

Australian gannet

Gannets dive into the ocean at speeds of **60 mph (95 kph).**

Long-tailed widow bird

Even with crazily long tail feathers, some birds **can still fly.**

This hummingbird can flap its wings up to **70 times per second.**

Marvelous spatuletail

HOW BIRDS FLY

Birds fly because they have wings. A bird can stay in the air, against the force of gravity, by flapping its pair of wings.

The shearwater's long wings let it **glide just above the waves** when it hunts.

This kestrel hovers with its **wings and tail spread** while looking for prey.

Common kestrel

Common tern

Sooty shearwater

PURPOSE OF FLIGHT

Birds don't just fly for the sheer fun of it! They fly to **escape enemies, chase after prey, and to migrate.**

Long wings and a forked tail make this bird **elegant and buoyant** in the air.

California condor

Hadada ibis

Strong fliers, dippers also use their wings to **swim underwater.**

Rhinoceros auklet

Mighty condors use their huge wings to **glide and soar.**

Gentoo penguin

This ibis **flaps a lot** using its super-broad wings.

White-throated dipper

Auks **furiously flap** their short wings to keep themselves aloft.

STYLES OF FLIGHT

Penguins are flightless birds, but their flipperlike wings let them **"fly" underwater.**

Birds fly in a variety of ways. They are able to **glide, flap, and soar** at different speeds.

More than a hundred pairs of weavers and their young can share their huge nests. Each family has its own chamber.

Sociable weaverbird

Amazing nests

Most bird species make nests, where they can **keep their eggs and young safe.** Nests are as diverse as birds themselves: they can be made out of all kinds of materials, and built in all sorts of strange places!

Birds as architects

Some nests look very delicate. They are in fact **incredibly strong** and can resist a lot of pulling and tugging. They often take a long time to make. Some birds build huge nests shared by many pairs and their young.

Male bowerbirds build fancy structures out of sticks. They decorate them with **bright objects** to attract females.

Great bowerbirds

Oropendolas build **dangly nests.** Many nests may hang from the same tree.

Montezuma oropendolas

Village weaver

A village weaver uses about **300 blades of grass and leaf strips** to build its nest.

This cave bird builds its nest out of layers of its **sticky saliva!**

Edible-nest swiftlet

White tern

This seabird **doesn't make a nest**—it lays its egg on a bare branch!

White storks

The perfect spot

Small birds tend to hide their nests in bushes and trees. Larger birds, however, often build big nests out in the open. They may use their nests for **years and years.**

The enormous nests built by storks can **weigh about as much as a horse!**

European robin

Peregrine falcons have **learned to nest on buildings** instead of cliffs.

Peregrine falcon

Robins love nesting in surprising **hiding spots,** where their young will be safe.

Manx shearwater

This seabird **nests in deep burrows,** which they only visit at night.

Eggs and chicks

All bird species lay eggs. The number of eggs the females lay varies by species. **Birds incubate their eggs.** This means they sit on the eggs to keep them warm until the chicks are ready to hatch.

Golden eagle

Tough eggs

Although eggs look fragile, they are **incredibly strong** since they need to protect the developing chick inside. But, of course, an egg will break if it falls!

Common ostrich

Birds that **nest in holes or burrows,** such as tawny owls and kiwis, often have white eggs.

Tawny owl

Here are the **largest and smallest bird eggs,** with a chicken egg for comparison.

Red grouse

Speckled eggs **blend in perfectly** with the ground around the nests.

Chicken

Bee hummingbird

Black-headed gull

Common quail

Great northern diver

Eurasian sparrowhawk

Great auk (extinct)

Desert lark

Newborn desert lark chicks have **hairlike feathers,** which help them keep cool.

Red-legged partridge

When partridge chicks hatch, they **already have feathers** and can run.

Types of chicks

Some chicks are born **covered with down** and can run and feed themselves. Others hatch naked and are totally dependent on their parents for weeks.

Kentish plover

Plover chicks are born with soft down and **strong, long legs.**

Bald eagles

Hoatzin

Hoatzin chicks have a **claw on each wing** to help them climb through branches.

Eaglets are born **weak and blind.** It's amazing that they grow up into such mighty birds!

13

This kite's hooked bill lets it **extract snails from their shells.**

Snail kite

What's on the menu?

Most birds are omnivores, which means they eat both animals and plants. Food gives birds the fuel to go about their lives and, importantly, the energy to fly, run, or swim. They find their food in a variety of ways.

Woodpeckers hammer on tree trunks with their bills to uncover **grubs.**

Great spotted woodpecker

This hawk uses its keen sight to **locate prey,** and its sharp talons to capture it.

Red-shouldered hawk

Goosander

Tiny teethlike projections on the edge of its bill help the goosander **grip slippery fish.**

Finding food

Birds use their sight to locate food. Some find food, such as fruit or insects, easily around them. Others have to search far and wide for their meals.

SEEDEATERS

Hawfinch

Most seedeaters, such as finches, have conical bills to help them crunch hard seeds.

INSECT EATERS

Mugimaki flycatcher

Insect eaters, such as flycatchers, have slim bills and feed exclusively on insects.

NECTAR FEEDERS

Sword-billed hummingbird

Hummingbirds are famous for poking their long bills inside flowers to drink the sweet nectar.

FISH CATCHERS

Little egret

Fish catchers, such as egrets, usually have long daggerlike bills to either stab or grab fish.

Birds have differently shaped bills depending on what they eat. Bills are lightweight and very important for helping birds get the right type of food.

PREDATORS

Eurasian sparrow hawk

Hawks and other hunters have strong, hooked bills for ripping the flesh of their prey.

PROBERS

Eurasian curlew

Probers, such as curlews, use their bills to probe muddy coastlines for invertebrates.

FRUIT EATERS

African gray parrot

Parrots have bills that are thick, hooked, and sharp, making them perfect for plucking fruit.

OTHER TYPES

Shoebill

Some birds' bills are highly specialized. For example, the shoebill uses its extraordinary bill to catch large river fish.

Incredible birds

Each one of the world's 10,500 bird species has its own special abilities and features that help it survive. Here are a few of Earth's most amazing, record-breaking birds.

Biggest

Common ostrich

An ostrich egg weighs the same as **24 chicken eggs.**

Smallest

Bee hummingbird

Nobody is sure why these birds bring rocks to their nests.

Strongest

Black wheatear

Biggest
Ostriches are the tallest and heaviest birds on Earth. They are native to Africa. Male ostriches can reach 9.2 ft (2.8 m) high—bigger than the world's tallest man.

Smallest
The bee hummingbird is the smallest bird in the world. It's even smaller than some insects! Males are about 2.2 in (5.5 cm) long, and females are slightly bigger.

Strongest
The black wheatear may be small, but it would win a gold medal for weight lifting in the bird world. The males carry rocks weighing up to two-thirds of their bodyweight to their nests.

Biggest
wingspan

Wandering albatross

These huge ocean birds can roam as far as **75,000 miles (120,000 km)** each year!

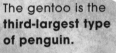

The gentoo is the **third-largest type of penguin.**

Fastest swimmer

Gentoo penguin

Fastest flier

Peregrine falcon

Biggest wingspan

The longest wings of the bird world belong to the wandering albatross. When fully outstretched, its wings can measure up to 11 ft (3.5 m) from tip to tip—the length of a small car.

Fastest swimmer

The gentoo penguin can't fly, but it's an amazing swimmer. Its top speed in the water is 22 mph (36 kph). That's about the same top speed as record-breaking sprinter, Usain Bolt!

Fastest flier

The peregrine falcon isn't just the fastest bird, it's the fastest animal in the world! When diving after prey, it reaches speeds up to 242 mph (390 kph)—faster than a Lamborghini car.

Macaws live in the wooded habitats of **South America**.

BIRD FAMILIES

All of the world's bird species can be grouped into different families based on the similarities they share.

Some birds in the same family are closely related, like the many species of colorful parrots. Other birds may look completely different and live in different habitats, even though they are part of the same family group. So while each family shares common characteristics, there are still **a lot of variety and loads of surprises** in each group.

Flightless birds

Most birds can fly, but there are more than 60 species that have lost the power of flight. **Flightless species evolved in environments where they didn't need to fly.** They often lived on islands where there were no predators.

Flightless cormorant

This island bird **uses its stunted wings to balance** as it jumps across coastal rocks.

Emperor penguin

Penguins have no need for flight because they are such superb aquatic birds. Emperors can dive deeper than any other bird.

EVOLUTION

Flightless bird species changed gradually, or evolved, over millions of years. This often happened when flying birds became isolated on islands. With no predators, and plenty of food, these birds had no need to fly anymore.

Even birds that can fly may also move around by walking or swimming.

This big duck uses its feet and small wings to **rapidly paddle** away from danger.

Falkland steamer duck

When running, emus flap their small wings to help **stabilize themselves.**

Emu

Common ostrich

This giant bird has **powerful legs** that make it a great runner—much faster than a human.

Macaroni penguin

Different bodies

Flightless birds are often large and heavy. This is because they no longer need to be **aerodynamic** and hollow boned for flight. Many have evolved strong legs for running.

Macaronis and other penguins still have **streamlined bodies and use their wings**—but for swimming rather than flying.

The largest species of kiwi, this heavy bird has **tiny wings.**

Great spotted kiwi

Young giant coots can fly, but they lose this ability as adults!

This endangered waterbird **lives in just one lake** in South America.

Junín grebe

Giant coot

The downside

Flightless birds can become well adapted to life in one place. But their populations can be **put at risk if anything changes** in their habitat, such as the arrival of humans.

Dodo

A relative of the pigeon, this large bird was **quickly wiped out** by hunters arriving on its island home.

Great auk

This Arctic seabird had few predators in its home, so **it wasn't afraid of humans.** It was hunted to extinction over a short period of time.

Wake Island rail

The Wake Island rail died out because it was **overhunted by soldiers** who came to its island home during World War II.

Game birds

This family is made of **short-winged, ground-loving birds.** Unfortunately for these handsome creatures, the word "game" in their name means that they are often hunted for sport or food.

Willow ptarmigan

Willow ptarmigans **turn white in winter** to match the snow of their alpine home.

Caucasian grouse

Male Caucasian grouse gather in **groups** to show off to females.

Spruce grouse

Helmeted guinea fowl

When humans approach this quail, **it freezes instead of flying away.**

Poor fliers

Almost no game birds can fly long distances. They usually keep to the ground, but they may **sleep** in trees.

Guinea fowl can fly, but **they usually walk instead.**

Montezuma quail

Domestic birds

Chickens were the first birds to be **domesticated by humans—about 8,000 years ago.** They provide a useful source of food.

Some quails are kept for eggs and meat. Others, such as California quails, are wild.

California quail

Turkey

Turkeys were domesticated **more than 2,000 years ago.**

Turkeys are the **heaviest game birds.**

Wild turkey

Staying safe

Since game birds aren't great fliers, they have other ways of **staying safe from predators.** They can be difficult to see because their plumage helps them camouflage, and they also tend to live in groups.

This type of pheasant is famed for the **fabulous tail of the male.**

Indian peafowl

Reeves's pheasant

This tragopan's diet is mostly **flowers, leaves, and grass.**

Swinhoe's pheasant

Temminck's tragopan

Congo peafowl

This widespread pheasant is **the most hunted bird in the world.**

Game birds and humans

Some game-bird species have been introduced in huge numbers so humans can hunt them freely. Others, however, are critically endangered.

Ring-necked pheasant

This bird is **very rare,** since it lives in dense jungles.

Cockerel

Like some other male game birds, cockerels have red flesh on their faces called "wattles."

Hens

Domestic hens have been raised over the years to **lay more eggs** than wild game birds.

Parrots

There are more than 350 species of parrot. They are often **vividly multicolored, and very noisy!** Some species only live in a small area, while others have been introduced around the world.

A world of parrots

When you think of wild parrots, you might imagine them squawking in the jungle. Parrots, however, also live in deserts, on mountains, and **even in cities.**

Yellow-chevroned parakeet

Spix's macaw

Red-and-green macaw

Male and female **macaws pair up for life.** They are also popular pets.

Yellow-billed parrot

Rainbow lorikeet

Monk parakeet

Austral parakeet

Green rosellas feed in both the forest **canopy and understory.**

Keas live in the mountains and include **meat in their diet.**

Kea

This South American bird lives the **farthest south** of any parrot species.

Green rosella

Amazing skills

Parrots have some incredible natural talents, like dexterity, long life spans, and intelligence. **They can learn complex tasks and even copy our speech!**

Golden parakeet

Pink cockatoo

Lovebirds are very affectionate and **become sick if separated** from their mates.

Fischer's lovebirds

Greater bluebonnet

Green and blue plumage helps this bird **hide in the foliage.**

Spectacled parrotlet

Vulturine parrot

Unusual parrots

Some parrots have surprising characteristics. Kakapos and night parrots are **nocturnal,** and vulturine parrots have **bald heads!**

Night parrot

Red-tailed black Cockatoo

Kakapo

This large parrot is **flightless,** and active only at night.

Philippine eagle

As its name suggests, this eagle mainly eats snakes.

Short-toed snake-eagle

This ferocious hawk feeds on small woodland animals.

Northern goshawk

Hunting techniques
Predators have **different hunting styles.** Some chase or pounce, while others search for dead animals.

Lappet-faced vulture

Also known as the **monkey-eating eagle,** this giant is the largest eagle on the planet.

Habitats
Birds of prey live in many habitats, from **Arctic regions to tropical jungles.** You'll find them in our own concrete jungles, too!

Secretary bird

This long-legged hunting bird kills reptiles by **stamping** on them!

Hunting birds

Often called "birds of prey," this group contains many different species. They are all predators, but have varied diets. Females are usually bigger than males and can hunt larger prey.

Steppe buzzard

This bird **migrates long distances** from eastern Europe and China to spend winters in Africa.

Spectacled owl

Bateleur

Little owl

An opportunistic hunter, this owl attacks any bird or small mammal that crosses its path.

Ural owl

Eastern screech-owl

This owl can be found in wooded areas even in the middle of cities.

Lesser kestrel

Lesser kestrels **hover in groups** looking for large insects.

People versus hunting birds

Unfortunately, birds of prey are often killed by humans because **they are seen as being a threat** to our domestic animals and livestock.

27

Waterbirds

The birds in this family spend their lives in or around water. Some have webbed feet and swim, while others wade in the water on long legs.

Canada goose

Pacific heron

Western Reef-heron

Mute swan

This heron is regularly **on the lookout** for wetlands in arid Australia.

Habitats
Waterbirds nest and feed in a number of habitats, from **coastlines and wetlands to lakes and rivers.** You'll find different birds in freshwater and saltwater habitats.

Mallard

African pygmy goose

Scarlet ibis

Northern shoveler

The beautiful, bright color of this bird's plumage comes from the **red shrimp and shellfish** it eats.

Wattled jacana

Horned grebe

This grebe eats its own feathers! They help the bird break down fish bones in its stomach.

Black-bellied whistling-duck

Unlike many other ducks, this species forms **pairs that stay together** for years.

Woodcock

Away from water

Some birds look like they belong in the waterbird family, but they don't live in watery habitats. Instead, they spend their lives in the middle of woods or in grasslands.

Diversity

Waterbirds vary greatly in size, from tiny shorebirds to enormous swans. Their bills may be short, long, or curved depending on what they eat.

Lesser flamingo

Flamingos suck water through their bills to **filter out small shrimp**.

Bar-tailed godwit

Godwits forage for invertebrates by **probing their long bills** into wet mud.

Seabirds

The birds in this family spend their whole lives out at sea, only coming onto land to raise their young. Some seabirds spend time in or on the water, while others just skim the surface to snatch food. Sadly, many of these great birds are at risk from human activities.

Atlantic puffin

Puffins' brightly colored bills become **small and gray** in the winter.

Life at sea
Seabirds have all kinds of skills to help them survive life at sea. They are fantastic **fliers, gliders, and fishers.** Some species are also able to dive very deep for fish.

The wandering albatross can **live for more than 50 years.**

Risks to seabirds
Overfishing by humans means that **some seabirds struggle to find enough food.** Pollution can cause seabirds to swallow pieces of plastic, while oil spills damage feathers and poison the birds.

These tiny seabirds have throat pouches, which they use for **storing crustacean prey.**

Wandering albatross

Magellanic diving-petrel

Little auks need to eat about **60,000 small crustaceans** every day.

Little auk

Northern gannet

Gannets **close their nostrils when diving** to prevent the salt water from getting in.

Some seabirds sweat sea salt from their nostrils!

Red-legged kittiwakes build **nests of mud, grass, and seaweed** on cliff ledges.

Red-legged kittiwake

Safety in numbers
Coming onto land is a **vulnerable time for seabirds.** The birds move awkwardly on solid ground, since they are better suited to the air or water. Their young also face danger from predators. This is why some seabird species nest in big colonies for protection.

This striking bird **lives in forests** and eats grasshoppers and beetles.

Banded broadbill

Two groups

Perching birds can be split into two groups. **Songbirds** make up one group. The birds in the other group **aren't great singers** and live mostly in the jungles of the Southern Hemisphere.

Bullfinches have a **food sac** in their mouth to bring food to their chicks.

Eurasian bullfinch

Perching birds

Also called passerines, perching birds make up more than half of the world's bird species. They are mostly small birds that spend a lot of time sitting in trees and shrubbery.

Part of the thrush family, this bird is mostly found in **mountain** areas.

White-throated sparrow

The song of this little bird sounds as though it's repeating the word **"Canada."**

This eye-catching bird sometimes makes its nests on **telephone poles.**

Ring ouzel

Scissor-tailed flycatcher

What is a perching bird?

The birds in this group have **four strong toes on each foot**—perfect for perching, or alighting on branches. Many are also celebrated songsters.

Superb fairywren

The males of this species sometimes pluck **yellow petals** to impress the females.

Mockingbirds can **mimic the calls** of many other birds— even hawks!

Northern mockingbird

When not breeding they can gather in flocks of up to **2,000 birds.**

More than half the world's bird species are passerines, and they are often the birds we know best.

Gouldian finch

Eurasian golden oriole

Orioles keep themselves to the **treetops,** rarely appearing out in the open.

Everywhere you look

Most of the birds that visit our backyards and parks are perching birds. **They are all around us.** Have you seen any today?

Common raven

Ravens are the **largest perching birds** in the world.

A member of the thrush family, this bird is a **symbol of spring** in many US states.

American robin

Wood warbler

This European species **migrates to Africa** for winter.

Unusual perching birds

Not all perching birds look the way you might expect! Some are large, such as ravens, while others **don't perch in trees at all!** There are also flamboyant-looking lyrebirds and rainbow-colored gems, such as Gouldian finches.

Hooded pitohui

Superb lyrebird

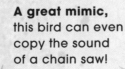

A great mimic, this bird can even copy the sound of a chain saw!

Predators beware! The plumage and skin of this bird are **poisonous.**

BIRD BEHAVIOR

Like humans, birds have a wide range of different behaviors to show their moods, attract mates, and defend themselves.

Birds are well known for a lot of things—such as singing, displays, and migrating—but why do they do these things? **Each species acts in its own way, different from even its close relatives.** That's why one of the many fascinating things about birds is watching how they behave, and figuring out what it means and why they do it.

When flocks of starlings gather, it's called a **murmuration.**

Amazonian umbrellabird

Rufous fantail

The rufous fantail **sings after sunset** to attract a mate.

Eurasian skylark

Skylarks' **songs may last many minutes.**

The songs of northern cardinals **vary from region to region.**

How do birds sing?

Songbirds have strong voices and **can breathe with one lung at a time,** so they don't have to pause for breath.

Eurasian bullfinch

Northern cardinal

Wood warbler

Male bullfinches may be very striking, but they have **very quiet and weak songs**.

River warbler

Songbird serenade

Songs are essential for birds to **recognize their owns species.** Females are attracted to males who sing loud and well, because they are signs of good health.

Singing

Birds are well known for their **amazing voices.** Many songbirds are small birds that use their voices to mark their territories, attract mates, or warn others to stay away.

Hazel grouse

These birds are now so rare that **young males can't find any adults** to teach them how to sing!

Regent honeyeater

Cedar waxwing

Learning to sing
Many birds are born knowing how to sing. Others have to learn their songs—they pick them up by listening to the older birds sing.

The robin is one of the few bird species where the **females sing, too.**

This secretive bird **sings with its tail raised** in dense undergrowth.

Siberian rubythroat

European robin

American goldfinch

Great spotted woodpecker

Unique voices
Each songbird species has its own voice. Some birds have incredibly loud songs that can be heard for miles. Others have quiet, **mechanical-sounding** songs.

37

A female greater bird-of-paradise **inspects the males** to see if she likes any of them.

World's greatest display

The male greater bird-of-paradise has the **most glamorous display in the bird world.** He freezes in motion with his head down, and elegant tail plumes upright.

Greater bird-of-paradise

Dazzling displays

One way that birds attract mates or warn rivals to stay away is by giving displays. This impressive behavior involves the bird **fluffing up its plumage to show off** its finery.

The male bird is still an **eye-catching sight** when it's not displaying.

When they display, the male birds gather in noisy, jostling groups and wait for the females to arrive.

More cool displays

Many male birds have **special feathers just for displaying**. The impressive plumes make them attractive to the females.

Great bustard

Male great bustards gather in groups on the plains, **puffing out their feathers.** They look huge beside the smaller females.

Ruff

Male ruffs show off their **incredible "necklace" of feathers** when they display. Each male has his own color pattern.

Indian peafowl

Peacocks (male peafowls) have around **150 eyespots** on their amazing tail feathers.

Camouflage

If a bird has plumage that blends in with its background, there is less chance that a hungry predator will find it. **Female birds are the masters of camouflage,** or blending in, so that they can protect their eggs and chicks.

SNOWY SCENERY

Snowy landscapes abound in polar, tundra, and mountainous regions. Birds that live in these places have **white plumage to blend in with the snow.**

Snowy owls' white feathers are **flecked with brown** to keep them camouflaged against snowy rocks.

Snowy owl

This lark lives in the northernmost parts of Africa and the Middle East.

Temminck's lark

DRY DESERTS

Desert birds are not very active during the heat of the day. To stay safe, they have **plumage that keeps them hidden against the sand and rocks.**

WONDERFUL WETLANDS

This important habitat is full of life, and it helps protect nearby land from floods. Wetland birds are often **brown to blend in with reeds and dry grasses.**

Bitterns have **streaky markings** to keep them well hidden in reed beds.

American bittern

Jacamars **sit and wait for insects** to fly past, before darting out to snap them up.

Green-tailed jacamar

FORESTS AND JUNGLES

Birds don't have to just be green to be camouflaged in a forest. As long as they stay still, **birds of any colors are hard to see among the plant life.**

Amazing journeys

The fact that birds can fly is fantastic enough, but **some go on amazing journeys, or migrations,** that may take them half way around the world. These journeys are even more astounding when you think how light birds are and how some species barely feed when traveling. What impressive stamina!

Common cuckoo

Male cuckoos may spend **just a few weeks** at breeding grounds in Europe before heading back to Africa.

This shy robin may **visit backyards** on its migration route.

Siberian blue robin

Bar-tailed godwit

This wader can fly for up to **nine days** without stopping!

Europe

Asia

Africa

Australasia

NW N NE
W E
SW SE
S

Navigation
Birds are born knowing where and when to travel. They navigate using the position of the sun, moon, and stars, as well as landmarks, such as rivers and mountains.

Many small birds **travel at night** to avoid predators. It's also cooler and usually less windy.

Why do birds migrate?

Birds migrate to avoid **bad weather and food shortages** that winter brings to the regions where they breed. Whole populations fly off to warmer areas where there is plenty to eat.

North America

Great shearwater

This seabird's migration route makes a **huge loop** around the Atlantic Ocean.

Preparing to travel

Birds change physically to prepare for their migration. Their hearts and flight muscles get bigger and stronger. They also gain weight—the fat will be used to fuel the flight.

The yellow warbler migrates across the **Gulf of Mexico** to South America.

South America

Yellow warbler

KEY

Common cuckoo

Siberian blue robin

Bar-tailed godwit

Yellow warbler

Great shearwater

This silent flier uses its **sharp claws** to attack any animal that ventures too close to its nest.

Tawny owl

Herring gulls enthusiastically defend their nests by **dive-bombing and pooping** on intruders.

European herring gull

Why defend a territory?

Birds defend their territories to stop other birds from feeding there—**they need the food for themselves** and their young. They will also drive out predators that enter their territory, usually to protect their eggs and chicks.

Northern flicker

A kick from a cassowary can **kill a person!** The bird's huge feet have a daggerlike claw on one toe.

Northern cassowary

Bird defenses

Many birds will try to fend off an enemy if they feel threatened. **Birds defend themselves in a variety of ways.** Some are aggressive, diving at intruders or striking them with their bills and claws. But others are sneaky, faking injuries to lure predators away from their young.

Food fights

Birds often squabble at feeders. It's usually the larger species that dominate, but once they've had their fill, the smaller species get a chance.

Blue jays can **mimic the sound of hawks** to clear bird trays for themselves!

Blue jays

Effective strategies

Different bird species often have their own strategies, or tactics, for **defending themselves or their young** from hungry predators.

Brown jay

Small flocks of brown jays **work together** to drive away large predators.

Meadow pipit

Meadow pipits fly excitedly just above your head to **lure you away** from their nests.

This large thrush often defends a bush **full of berries** from other birds!

Mistle thrush

Long-eared owl

Owlets **puff themselves up** to try and look fearsome in the face of danger.

After dark

Bird species that are active after dark are called nocturnal birds. The best known of these are owls, but there are others, such as nightjars, that also hunt at night. Nighttime is also a good time for smaller birds to migrate—as long as they don't bump into any owls!

Male nightingales **sing at night** to attract females flying overhead.

Common nightingale

Australian owlet-nightjar

This tiny bird **dives from its perch** to snatch nocturnal insects.

During the day

Nocturnal birds usually hide in trees during the day. They can sleep safe and sound from predators because they are so well camouflaged by their brown plumage.

Night migrations

Many bird species migrate at night. Flying across cooler, calmer skies uses less energy. On clear nights, the birds can use the **stars to guide them** on their journey.

Redwing

Unusually for migrating birds, redwings **rarely return to the same area** each winter.

Fieldfares are not nocturnal, but they migrate at night in the spring and fall.

Fieldfare

White-fronted scops owl

Little is known about this rare owl, whose **forest home** is slowly being destroyed.

Spotted nightjar

Nighttime adaptations

Many nocturnal birds have incredible night vision, with big eyes to catch any glimmer of light. They also fly silently and have a **superb sense of hearing** to help them locate their prey.

Nightjars spend the day **on the ground,** blending in with their surroundings.

Stunning spectacles

Birds are fascinating creatures that sometimes gather in enormous flocks to feed, roost, or migrate. These gatherings make amazing spectacles to watch and enjoy.

A gathering of flamingos is known as a "flamboyance."

FLAMINGO FLOCKS

Greater flamingos live their entire lives in flocks in saltwater wetlands. To see vast numbers of these tall, graceful birds in an estuary is an **unforgettable experience!**

Greatest flocks of all time

The passenger pigeon was **the most abundant bird ever to live.** The species migrated across eastern North America in flocks so huge that they would take days to pass overhead. Despite their numbers, the passenger pigeon became extinct in the early 20th century, mostly due to overhunting.

49

BIRD HABITATS

Birds make their homes in many different habitats—places that provide enough food for them to survive and raise their young.

Birds have adapted to most areas of the planet. Their habitats include forests, shores, deserts, cities, and even underground! Some species are very specialized and can live in only one type of habitat. Others are more general and can survive in more than one place.

For these oystercatchers, the sandy shores and coastal wetlands provide **a lot of food buried under the soft ground.**

Wet mountainous forests are the home of this insect eater.

Long-billed woodcreeper

Although small, roadside hawks often catch **little monkeys.**

Roadside hawk

Rufous-backed antvireo

This woodcreeper sometimes forages in the trees **in pairs.**

To flush out insects hiding under tree bark, this nuthatch will flap its wings vigorously.

Tropical forests

The forests in hot tropical regions of the world **cover more of Earth than any other type of forest.** No wonder so many of the world's birds live here!

Velvet-fronted nuthatch

Pittas are secretive tropical forest birds that are rarely seen.

Blond-crested woodpecker

There are plenty of ants—this woodpecker's favorite food—in its tropical forest home.

Superb pitta

Forest living

Birds that live in forests are often noisy. However, they can be **difficult to see among the foliage,** despite some being brightly colored. There are different types of forests, and birds have adapted to each kind in different ways.

This species of woodpecker **often feeds on the forest floor,** not just on tree trunks.

Northern flicker

Temperate forests are rich in food, which is why this small bird never travels far from where it was born.

The black-and-white warbler **hunts for its food** on tree trunks and branches.

White-throated treecreeper

Black-and-white warbler

Adult pairs of this bird **smear insects** around the entrance of their nest holes to discourage squirrels from entering.

White-breasted nuthatch

White-cheeked nuthatch

Temperate forests
Temperate forests grow in the milder parts of the world. Many of the birds in these forests migrate south for the winter when it gets cold.

Tiny and crepuscular, the pygmy owl is a **voracious predator** of small birds.

This nuthatch hunts for food on the underside of **lichen-draped** branches.

Pygmy owl

Boreal forests
These enormous forests cover the **cold northerly areas of the world** toward the Arctic. They are home to many birds, including breeding waders—some of which nest in trees.

Connecticut warbler

Sikkim treecreeper

This shy songbird forages on the ground in **dense vegetation.**

This bird has recently been recognized as a **new species.**

53

A penguin's black-and-white coloring is called countershading. This pattern makes it harder for the penguin to be seen from both above and below when it's swimming. In this way, it's hidden from predators and can sneak up on prey.

Frozen home

Antarctica is the coldest place on Earth, and the wildlife that lives on and around this icy continent has **adapted to the harsh conditions.** The chinstrap penguin is one of the birds that has managed to thrive in the extreme climate.

Nests

Different penguins have different types of nesting habits. Chinstrap penguins build very simple nests from **a pile of rocks.**

Male and female chinstrap penguins **take turns incubating** their two eggs.

Male chinstrap penguins have been known to form pairs and **try to raise young,** too.

Every day, the chinstrap penguin swims up to 50 miles (80 km) offshore to catch seafood.

Climate change

The Earth's atmosphere has been slowly getting warmer since the 19th century due to human activities. This has caused changes in the climate around the world, including Antarctica. **Enormous areas of ice are melting,** which affects where penguins can nest.

Surviving the cold

Chinstrap penguins have a thick waterproof coat and blubber to keep them warm and dry. They also have **special blood vessels** in their wings and legs that help them keep heat inside their bodies.

Chicks

Chinstrap penguin chicks spend about a month in their nest. They then join other young chinstraps in a big group called a **crèche.**

Penguin chicks are **fat and fluffy** to help them keep warm.

At about two months old, the chicks lose their down and **grow adult feathers.** They are then ready to go in the ocean.

Tufted puffins

These puffins may dig their own burrow, or use natural holes in rocky cliffs.

African harrier-hawk

This predator often walks around **looking for burrows.**

Predators

Birds aren't always safe underground. Some smaller predators, such as snakes and weasels, will **raid burrows** to eat the eggs or chicks they find there.

Birds underground

No bird spends its entire life below ground, but **several species do nest underground.** Some dig their own homes, while others use natural holes or the abandoned homes of other animals.

Burrowing owl

Since this owl likes open landscapes, it sometimes moves into the grassy areas of **airports!**

Why nest in burrows?
Burrows are safe places for young birds, and they give protection against cold weather and predators.

Making burrows

Animals such as reptiles and mammals have handy paws and claws, so it's easy for them to dig. Birds have to use their bills and feet—it's a tough job!

Southern carmine bee-eaters

This attractive bird digs **long burrows** in vertical mud banks.

Borrowing burrows

Digging burrows is hard work for birds, and it may injure them. For these reasons, birds sometimes use **old burrows dug by other animals.**

White-browed tit

This perching bird sometimes raises its young in **the old burrows of rodents.**

Crab-plover

Until they can walk, crab-plover chicks stay in their **safe and cosy burrows.**

Crab-plover burrows

Crab-plovers are the only burrowing wading bird. **Their burrows are the ideal temperature for incubating eggs,** so parents can leave them and look for food.

Kelp goose

This goose **eats only kelp,** which is a type of seaweed.

Least tern

Coastlines are very important **nesting areas** for colonies of this tiny tern.

On the coast

These habitats are a **vital source of food and nesting areas** for a large number of coastal birds.

Pacific reef heron

This heron sometimes **dangles its toes** in coastal waters to attract fish.

Coastal life

Our coastlines can be very busy places, with many types of birds **taking advantage of the abundance of food.** Some birds wade or dive for food, while others probe the sand and rocks.

Caspian plovers often **nest in dry grasslands** miles from the coast, where they feed.

Female rock pipits use **seaweed and grass** to make their nests.

Rock pipit

Caspian plover

This plover nests on beaches in North America and is **easily disturbed** by human activities.

Piping plover

Coastlines in danger

Our planet has many thousands of miles of coastline. Sadly for birds, **many coastline habitats are now polluted or have been destroyed.**

Long bills help wading birds probe for deep-burrowing shrimp and crabs.

Although they are waders, these avocets have partially **webbed feet** and are good swimmers.

American avocets

Long-billed curlew

Male long-billed curlews are smaller than the females, and usually spend the most time raising the chicks.

Wrybill

Wrybills use their unique bills, which **bend to the right,** to pry prey from under rocks.

What to eat?

A healthy coast contains millions of crustaceans, wormlike creatures, and other invertebrates. They provide a **bountiful source of food** for birds.

59

Desert survivors

Desert birds are highly specialized. They have adapted to **life away from water** and in intense heat. The crowned sandgrouse is one species that has learned to live in extreme desert conditions.

This sandgrouse **avoids areas with a lot of plants** because predators may be lurking there.

There are **16 species of sandgrouse,** but only the crowned sandgrouse lives in these tough desert habitats.

Sandgrouse family

Nobody is really sure which birds are the sandgrouse's closest relatives. At different times, scientists have tried to slot them into the grouse, pigeon, and wader families. It's still a mystery, however, and sandgrouse now make up a bird family of their own.

Crowned sandgrouse are hard to detect because their plumage matches the sandy desert landscape.

During the day

In the daytime—under the blazing desert sun—sandgrouse quietly **search for seeds.** They may gather in flocks of up to 100 birds.

The male sandgrouse's belly feathers have **adapted** to soak up and hold water.

Giving chicks water

When visiting water holes, male sandgrouse soak up water with their belly feathers. They then fly back to their chicks, which sip the water from the feathers.

Birdhouses are great for urban birds. For species that are in decline, such as the purple martin, it can even help them bounce back.

Purple martin

Urban homes

In urban areas, some birds can find spots that are similar to their natural habitats. Flat **gravel roofs are like coastlines** to gulls, and skyscrapers are like cliffs to peregrine falcons.

Life in the city

Cities may be full of people, but **birds can still live there, too.** They make their homes in scattered areas of woods, lakes, rivers, parks, grasslands, and even on buildings.

This wader has taken to **nesting on flat roofs** in cities such as Cairo, Egypt.

Senegal thick-knee

Magpie-larks are very social, chatty birds, but their **shrieking** can be quite annoying to their human neighbors!

Easier to see

Birds living in towns and cities are often **easy to approach** since they are used to us being around. In the countryside, birds are much shyer.

Tufted titmouse

Small and **very curious,** titmice sometimes sit on windowsills and look into houses!

Magpie-lark

Did you know?

About 20 percent of all bird species are able to live in urban areas. Thanks to the variety of habitats in our cities, many birds can find homes among us.

Bogota rail

The best place to see this **threatened waterbird** is in marshy areas in the city of Bogotá, Colombia.

63

Binoculars are a key tool for bird-watchers. They allow you to see birds in much more detail.

BIRDS AND ME

Birds are wonderful creatures that enrich our lives. They are all around us, and easy to see.

Birds have featured in our history, culture, and folklore since the first humans walked the Earth. They have captivated us with their plumage, songs, and their ability to fly. It hasn't always been a good relationship, however, since we have hunted many species to extinction. Now more than ever it's important to learn about birds, and help protect their ways of life.

Birds and us

Birds are **symbols of freedom,** and yet we have always wanted to control and tame them. People around the world have found different ways to use birds to help us in our lives.

Red junglefowl

Domestic birds

Humans have been domesticating birds for **thousands of years.** Some, such as chickens, are kept as sources of food. Many are pets loved for their singing skills or ability to mimic us. Others, such as peafowl, are allowed to roam freely as ornaments.

Chickens are very **smart birds** and have great memories.

Domestic chicken

Native to Asia, the red junglefowl is the **ancestor of the domestic chicken.**

Working birds

Humans have put birds to work in a variety of ways over the centuries. They carry messages, fish, and even control the numbers of other birds for us.

Harris's hawk

Harris's hawks are used to **chase pigeons away** from airport runways and city centers.

Messenger pigeon

Pigeons have often been used in wars to **carry messages** over enemy lines.

Japanese cormorant

People have used cormorants to **catch fish** for hundreds of years.

Pet birds

We keep a variety of birds as pets—from canaries and finches to parrots and owls. They usually live their **whole lives in cages** or larger enclosures called aviaries.

African gray parrot

Parrots are popular pets because of their colorful feathers and ability to **mimic human speech.**

Plant pollinators

Some birds drink nectar from flowers. By visiting a lot of flowers, the birds help spread the flowers' pollen. The plants then use this pollen to make new seeds. **Animals that spread pollen are called pollinators.**

Northern rosella

Bearded mountaineer

Hummingbirds can drink **their weight in nectar** in a single day.

Spreading seeds

Many birds eat fruit and nuts that contain seeds. The seeds **travel through the birds' digestive systems** before passing out in their droppings. These seeds can then grow into new plants, such as flowers and trees.

Ruby-throated hummingbird

Cleaning up

Some birds are scavengers—they eat animals that are already dead. Scavengers help keep ecosystems tidy by eating up dead animals that might spread disease.

White-headed vulture

Birds and the planet

Vultures are scavengers that use their **keen eyesight** to spot dead animals from the air.

Pest control

Birds that eat insects can help keep pests under control. Without these birds, whole fields of **crops could be destroyed** by insects.

White-throated bee-eater

Helping the reef

Seabirds travel over the ocean and coastlines, pooping as they fly. All this **bird poop contains nitrogen,** which plantlike algae in the ocean need to grow. Algae-eating fish living on reefs with seabirds nearby grow faster and larger than fish at reefs without birds.

Red-footed boobies

Working together

Some animals can help each other out. This partnership is called **a symbiotic relationship.** Honeyguides show honey badgers where bees live. The badgers then eat the bees' honey, and the birds eat the dead bees that are left behind.

Greater honeyguide

Birds interact with plants and other animals in all kinds of helpful ways. Without these brilliant birds, our planet would be a very different place.

Birds at risk

Birds are very sensitive to the actions of humans. As our population grows, birds face more and more threats, especially habitat loss. Many species are in need of immediate help or they'll become lost to us forever.

Spoon-billed sandpiper

Sandpipers raised in captivity have been **released into the wild** to boost the numbers of this endangered wader.

People were **banned from hunting** this small bird, so its numbers have begun to increase again.

Yellow-breasted bunting

Conservation

Many people around the world are trying to protect birds. We can do this by **creating nature reserves** where birds can thrive, and asking hunters not to kill threatened species.

Extinct in the wild due to **deforestation,** this beautiful parrot now exists only in captivity.

Spix's macaw

The emperor penguin's icy Antarctic habitat is slowly melting due to **climate change.**

Emperor penguins

Threatened

Many bird species are under threat of extinction. The reasons for this include habitat loss, climate change, the wild-bird trade, and overhunting. Humans need to change their relationship with the natural world to help these birds survive.

There are **only about 300** Bali mynas left in the wild. Many are illegally trapped and sold as pets.

Bali myna

European turtle-dove

Hunters shoot this bird **during its migration,** and it's now close to extinction.

Helping birds

It's easy to help the birds in your neighborhood. You can provide them with food or a safe place to nest. This not only benefits the birds, but also gives you the opportunity to see these beautiful creatures up close every day.

Different types of bird food will attract a **variety of birds.**

Birdhouses are great for bird species that **nest in holes.**

Nuts and seeds attract seedeaters, while a pine cone **filled with suet** tempts insect eaters.

BUILD A BIRDHOUSE

Ask an adult to help you build a birdhouse. Make sure it's waterproof, and use natural materials and colors. The entrance should not face direct sunlight, because this might overheat the birds inside.

MAKE A BIRD FEEDER

You can make a simple bird feeder out of an old milk or juice carton. Cut holes in the sides, and fill the bottom of the feeder with **seeds, nuts, mealworms, or suet.** Just make sure you hang it somewhere that cats can't reach the feeding birds!

Hummingbirds love sugar water. To make it, mix four cups of water with one cup of sugar.

To stay healthy, birds need to **drink and bathe** in water.

There are many different styles of window decals to help **stop birds from flying into the glass.** Stripes, squares, and birds of prey are popular choices.

Window decal

CREATE A BIRDBATH

Use a shallow dish (no deeper than 1 in/2.5 cm) or a trash-bin lid turned upside down, supported by bricks. **Put it out in the open,** so the birds using it can see if enemies approach. Make sure you clean and refill it regularly.

PREVENT WINDOW STRIKES

Window strikes kill millions of birds every year. You can help prevent this by sticking special stickers, called "decals," on your windows. The decals break up the reflection in the glass, so birds won't try to fly through it.

Birding

Birds are everywhere. If you keep your eyes open and listen, you'll come across many species in your neighborhood. They're often easy to see in urban areas because they're used to people. Take a look out of your window. What birds can you see?

House martin

In Europe, northern Africa, and northern Asia, house martins sometimes nest **under roof eaves.**

Find a local spot

Make a nearby green space your local spot. Visit it often—at different times of the day—and in time **you'll discover all the different birds** that feed and nest in your area.

Find your nearest pond, lake, river, or canal and **see what waterbirds you can spot.**

This falcon often **perches on the ledges of tall buildings.** It is found in many countries around the world.

Peregrine falcon

Red or pink perching birds are colorful, but they can be **hard to spot** against brown tree branches. Take your time and look closely.

In eastern Asia, you might see a varied tit **in the bushes** of parks and yards.

Varied tit

Photographing birds

Photos are a great way to **catalogue local birds.** Practice taking pictures with your phone or a camera. You'll soon have that perfect shot!

As you watch birds, you'll discover many **fascinating things** about their habits and behavior.

How to be a birder

It's easy to start your new birding adventure! Bring a pair of binoculars so you can watch the birds from afar without disturbing them. A phone and notebook can help you record your discoveries. And don't forget a coat and sturdy shoes in case it rains.

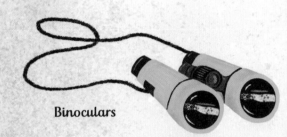

Binoculars

Notebook and pen

Raincoat and sturdy shoes

Cell phone

National birds

Many nations have chosen a national bird to represent their country. It could be a bird that's important in their folklore. Or perhaps the bird reveals what type of environments the country has. It could be a rare bird found only in this one place. Or it may just be because people love that local species! Here are some of the beloved bird symbols chosen around the world.

(U) = unofficial

Afghanistan Golden eagle
Andorra Bearded vulture (U)
Angola Red-crested turaco
Anguilla (UK) Zenaida dove
Antigua and Barbuda Magnificent frigatebird
Argentina Rufous hornero
Aruba (Netherlands) Brown-throated parakeet
Australia Emu (U)
Austria Barn swallow
Bahamas American flamingo
Bahrain Himalayan bulbul
Bangladesh Oriental magpie-robin
Belgium Eurasian kestrel
Belize Keel-billed toucan
Bermuda (UK) Bermuda petrel
Bhutan Common raven
Bolivia Andean condor

Bonaire (Netherlands) American flamingo
Botswana Kori bustard
Brazil Rufous-bellied thrush
British Virgin Islands (UK) Mourning dove
Canada Canadian jay (U)
Cayman Islands (UK) Grand Cayman parrot
Chile Andean condor
China Red-crowned crane (U)
Colombia Andean condor
Costa Rica Clay-colored thrush
Cuba Cuban trogon
Denmark Mute swan
Dominica Imperial parrot
Dominican Republic Palmchat
Ecuador Andean condor

El Salvador Turquoise-browed motmot
Estonia Barn swallow
Finland Whooper swan (U)
France Gallic rooster (domestic chicken) (U)
Germany Golden eagle (U)
Grenada Grenada dove
Guatemala Resplendent quetzal
Guyana Hoatzin
Haiti Hispaniolan trogon
Iceland Gyrfalcon
India Indian peafowl
Indonesia Javan hawk-eagle
Iraq Chukar
Israel Hoopoe
Italy Italian sparrow (U)
Jamaica Red-billed streamertail

Japan Green pheasant
Jordan Sinai rosefinch
Kenya Lilac-breasted roller (U)
Latvia White wagtail
Liberia Common bulbul
Lithuania White stork
Luxembourg Goldcrest
Malaysia Rhinoceros hornbill
Malta Blue rock-thrush
Mexico Crested caracara
Mongolia Saker falcon
Montserrat (UK) Montserrat oriole
Myanmar/Burma Gray peacock-pheasant (U)
Namibia African fish eagle
Nepal Himalayan monal
Netherlands Black-tailed godwit
New Zealand North Island brown kiwi (U)
Nicaragua Turquoise-browed motmot
Nigeria Black crowned crane
North Korea Northern goshawk
Northern Mariana Islands (US) Mariana fruit-dove
Norway White-throated dipper
Pakistan Chukar
Palau Palau fruit-dove

Palestine Palestine sunbird (U)
Panama Harpy eagle
Papua New Guinea Raggiana bird-of-paradise
Paraguay Bare-throated bellbird
Peru Andean cock-of-the-rock
Philippines Philippine eagle
Poland White-tailed eagle
Puerto Rico (US) Puerto Rican spindalis (U)
Qatar Saker falcon
Romania Great white pelican (U)
Saint Helena (UK) St. Helena plover
Saint Kitts and Nevis Brown pelican
Saint Lucia St. Lucia parrot
Saint Vincent and the Grenadines St. Vincent parrot
Samoa Tooth-billed pigeon
Saudi Arabia Saker falcon
Seychelles Seychelles parrot
Singapore Crimson sunbird (U)
South Africa Blue crane
South Korea Oriental magpie (U)
South Sudan African fish eagle

Spain Spanish eagle (U)
Sri Lanka Sri Lankan junglefowl
Sweden Eurasian blackbird (U)
Suriname Lesser kiskadee
Thailand Siamese fireback
Trinidad and Tobago
  Trinidad Scarlet ibis
  Tobago Rufous-vented chachalaca
Turkey Redwing
Turks and Caicos (UK) Brown pelican
Uganda Gray crowned-crane
United Arab Emirates Peregrine falcon
United Kingdom
  England European robin (U)
  Northern Ireland Northern lapwing (U)
  Scotland Golden eagle (U)
  Wales Red kite (U)
United States of America Bald eagle
US Virgin Islands (US) Bananaquit
Venezuela Venezuelan troupial
Zambia African fish-eagle
Zimbabwe African fish-eagle

Glossary

ADAPT
How a living thing changes over time to help it survive better in its environment.

BILL
The jaws of a bird. Also known as a beak.

BIRD
Warm-blooded animal with a backbone, bill, and feathers.

CAMOUFLAGE
Colors or patterns on an animal's skin, fur, or feathers that help it blend in with its environment.

CARNIVORE
Animal that eats meat.

CLIMATE CHANGE
Change in temperature and weather across the Earth. It could be natural or caused by human activity, such as pollution.

CONSERVATION
Protecting environments and wildlife.

CREPUSCULAR
Active at twilight.

DEFORESTATION
Cutting down trees and destroying forests.

DOMESTICATED
Animals kept as pets or on farms.

DOWN
A layer of soft, fluffy feathers that provide good insulation.

ENDANGERED
When an animal or plant species is in danger of dying out.

EVOLVE
The way living things change and adapt over time to help them survive.

EXTINCT
A plant or animal species that has no living members.

FORAGE
When animals search for food.

HABITAT
Area where an animal or plant lives.

INCUBATE
Keeping eggs warm until they hatch.

INVERTEBRATE
Animal that does not have a backbone, such as an insect or crustacean.

MIGRATION
Seasonal or periodic movement by animals to a different region.

MOLT
When a bird loses its feathers and grows new ones.

NATIVE
Species that have always lived in an area, rather than ones that have been introduced.

NOCTURNAL
Active at night.

OMNIVORE
Animal that eats both plants and meat.

PLUMAGE
All of a bird's feathers.

POLLEN
Powder that comes from flowering plants.

PREDATOR
Animal that hunts other living animals for food.

PREY
Animal that is hunted by another animal for food.

SCAVENGER
Animal that feeds on the remains of dead animals.

SPECIES
Specific types of animals or plants with shared features that can produce young together.

SYMBIOTIC
A type of relationship where different living things can benefit and help each other.

TERRITORY
Area that an animal considers its own and that it will defend from others.

URBAN
Built-up area, such as in a city or a large town.

Index

Acknowledgements

The publisher would like to thank the following people for their assistance: Caroline Twomey for proofreading; Helen Peters for the index; Neeraj Bhatia and Jagtar Singh for image work; and Sakshi Saluja for picture research.

PICTURE CREDITS

The publisher would like to thank the following for their kind permission to reproduce their photographs: (Key: a-above; b-below/bottom; c-center; f-far; l-left; r-right; t-top)

1 Dreamstime.com: Designprintck (background). 2-3 Dreamstime.com: Designprintck (background). 4-5 Dreamstime.com: Martin Pelanek. 5 Dreamstime.com: Designprintck (background). 6 Dorling Kindersley: Peter Minister (clb). Dreamstime.com: Chernetskaya (bl). 7 Dorling Kindersley: Jerry Young (bc). Dreamstime.com: Atman (tc); Jessamine (tr); Svetlana Foote (bl). 8 Getty Images: 500px Prime / Johnny Kääpä. 9 Alamy Stock Photo: AGAMI Photo Agency / Dubi Shapiro (cla); blickwinkel / Woike (t); AGAMI Photo Agency / Karel Mauer (cb); All Canada Photos / Tim Zurowski (fcrb). Depositphotos Inc: DennisJacobsen (tl). Dorling Kindersley: Bill Schmoker (clb). Dreamstime.com: Designprintck (background); Kinnon / Woravit Vijitpanya (bl). Getty Images: 500Px Plus / Kári Kolbeinsson (tc/gannet); Corbis Documentary / Arthur Morris (cr). Getty Images: E+ / Andyworks (cl); OldFulica (cb/condor). naturepl.com: 2020VISION / Andy Rouse (crb). Shutterstock.com: WesselDP (tr). 10 Alamy Stock Photo: Minden Pictures / Gerry Ellis (bc). Dreamstime.com: Altaoosthuizen (cla); Rainer Lesniewski (t); Nickolay Stanev (bl). 11 123RF.com: Eric Isselee (cr). Alamy Stock Photo: blickwinkel / K. Wothe (tr, tr/eggs); FLPA (br). Dreamstime.com: Necati Bahadir Bermek (clb); Douglas Olivares (tl); Andrey Eremin (bc); Isselee (cl). Shutterstock.com: Rob Jansen (cla). SuperStock: NHPA (cra). 12-13 Dreamstime.com: Designprintck (background). 13 Alamy Stock Photo: manjeet & yograj jadeja (t); Nature Picture Library / Hanne & Jens Eriksen (clb); Minden Pictures / Flip de Nooyer (cb). Dreamstime.com: Víctor Suárez Naranjo (c). Getty Images: Design Pics / Its About Light (crb). 14 123RF.com: ajt / Andrzej Tokarski (bc, clb). Dorling Kindersley: E. J. Peiker (moorhen x2). Dreamstime.com: Eng101 (cl); Dan Rieck (c); Tom Meaker (tl). 15 Dreamstime.com: Designprintck (background). 16 Alamy Stock Photo: robertharding / Michael Nolan (c). Dreamstime.com: Joan Egert (cb); Igor Stramyk (cl); Javier Alonso Huerta (crb). 16-17 Dreamstime.com: Designprintck (background). 17 Dreamstime.com: Sergey Korotkov (c); Julienne Spiteri (cb); Tarpan (ca); Sederi (cl). FLPA: (cr). 18-19 Dreamstime.com: Yongkiet. 19 Dreamstime.com: Designprintck (background). 20 Alamy Stock Photo: All Canada Photos / Glenn Bartley (br); Krystyna Szulecka (cla). Dorling Kindersley: Will Heap / Peter Warren (t). Dreamstime.com: Jan Martin Will (cr). 20-21 Dreamstime.com: Designprintck (background). 21 Alamy Stock Photo: imageBROKER / Erhard Nerger (c); simon margetson travel (cl); imageBROKER / Wilfried Wirth (tr); Nature Picture Library / Tui De Roy (cb/kiwi). Depositphotos Inc: imagebrokermicrostock (bc). Dorling Kindersley: Cecil Williamson Collection (cb); Natural History Museum, London (cr). Dreamstime.com: Steveheap (c/rocks). 22 Alamy Stock Photo: All Canada Photos / Ron Erwin (cr); Bill Gozansky (clb); Nature Photographers Ltd / Brian E Small (crb). Dorling Kindersley: Barrie Watts (grass). Dreamstime.com: Vasiliy Vishnevskiy (tr). 22-23 Dreamstime.com: Designprintck (b/background). 23 Alamy Stock Photo: Ernie Janes (c). Dreamstime.com: Ahkenahmed (tl); Dewins (palm leaves); Mikelane45 (cl); Anne Coatesy (clb); Wrangel (crb). 24 123RF.com: julinzy (tr). Alamy Stock Photo: CTK (cb); Dave Watts (br/rosella). Dreamstime.com: Chernetskaya (br); Vaclav Matous (cl). 24-25 Dreamstime.com: Dewins (tc). 25 123RF.com: lightwise (jungle background); rodho (bl); Dmitry Pichugin (tl). Alamy Stock Photo: blickwinkel / McPHOTO / DIZ (cb); imageBROKER / GTW (bl/parakeet). Dorling Kindersley: Mona Dennis (c). Dreamstime.com: Dewins (cra); Taweesak Sriwannawit (bc). Getty Images / iStock: nmulconray (cl). 26 Alamy Stock Photo: blickwinkel / McPHOTO / PUM (cr); Estan Cabigas (cla). Dorling Kindersley: The National Birds of Prey Centre (br). 27 Alamy Stock Photo: Biosphoto / Saviero Gatto (bl). Dreamstime.com: Altaoosthuizen (cla). Getty Images / iStock: Jens_Lambert_Photography (crb). 28 Dorling Kindersley: Jerry Young (br); Peter Anderson (clb). Dreamstime.com: Alfotokunst (cr); Martin Pelanek (cla); Fischer0182 (clb/shoveler); Mikelane45 (bc); Mexrix (sea); Charles Brutlag (tr). 29 Dorling Kindersley: Jerry Young (br). Dreamstime.com: Dule964 (autumn leaves); Howléwu (tc); Viter8 (cr); Paul Reeves (bc). Fotolia: Yong Hian Lim (cr/palm trees). 30 123RF.com: Aleksey Poprugin (blue plastic bag). Dreamstime.com: Costasz (blue bottle); Vladvitek (cla); Melonstone (cra); Dalia Kvedaraite (tr); Alfio Scisetti (green bottles x2); Lemusique (plastic bag); Gamjai / Penchan Pumila (yellow cap bottle). Getty Images / iStock: mzphoto11 (bc). 31 Alamy Stock Photo: FLPA (br). Getty Images / iStock: Gerald Corsi (tl); mauribo (tc). 32 123RF.com: Thawat Tanhai (tl). Depositphotos Inc: mikelane45 (crb). Dorling Kindersley: E. J. Peiker (clb). Dreamstime.com: Sandi Cullifer (br); Brian Kushner (cl); Paddyman2013 (bl). 33 Dorling Kindersley: Mike Lane (cb). Dreamstime.com: Eng101 (tr); Farinoza (cra); Petar Kremenarov (ca). naturepl.com: Daniel Heuclin (crb). 34-35 Getty Images: AFP / Menahem Kahana. 35 Dreamstime.com: Atman (b); Designprintck (background); Vasyl Helevachuk (br). 36 Alamy Stock Photo: FLPA (tl). Dreamstime.com: Charles Brutlag (cra); Imogen Warren (tc); Keithpritchard (tr); Kaido Rummel (cl); Volodymyr Kucherenko (br). 37 Dreamstime.com: Agami Photo Agency (clb); Mikalay Varabey (tl); Hernani Jr Canete (ca); Ken Griffiths (tr); Ruhuntn (cb); Vasyl Helevachuk (br). 38-39 Shutterstock.com: simibonay. 39 Alamy Stock Photo: Alessandro Mancini (bc). Dorling Kindersley: Markus Varesvuo (cra). Dreamstime.com: Volodymyr Byrdyak (cra); Iakov Filimonov (br). 40 Dorling Kindersley: Peter Anderson (stones). Dreamstime.com: Agami Photo Agency (tl). 41 Alamy Stock Photo: imageBROKER / Wilfried Wirth (western sword fern). Dreamstime.com: Frankjoe1815 (crb); Brian Lasenby (l). 42 123RF.com: Dennis Jacobsen (crb). Dreamstime.com: Dennis Jacobsen (cla); Prin Pattawaro (cra). 42-43 Dreamstime.com: Ruslanchik / Ruslan Nassyrov (background). 43 Dorling Kindersley: NASA (tr). Dreamstime.com: Paul Reeves (bc); Harold Stiver (cr). 44 Dreamstime.com: Hellmann1 (bl); Isselee (tr). Getty Images: Tier Und Naturfotografie J und C Sohns (tl). naturepl.com: Alex Mustard (c). 45 Alamy Stock Photo: Minden Pictures / Jim Brandenburg (c). Dreamstime.com: Linnette Engler (cra); Mikelane45 (cr, bc); Slowmotiongli (crb). 46 Alamy Stock Photo: Auscape International Pty Ltd / Robert McLean (bl); Biosphoto / Mario Cea Sanchez (cb). 46-47 123RF.com: citadelle (cb). 47 Dorling Kindersley: NASA (tr). Dreamstime.com: Per Grunditz (clb); Zeytun Images (clb/nightjar). Getty Images / iStock: A-Digit (tc); MikeLane45 (ca); Thipwan (br). 48-49 Dreamstime.com: Davide Guidolin. 50-51 Shutterstock.com: Wang LiQiang. 51 Dreamstime.com: Designprintck (background). 52 Alamy Stock Photo: Nature Picture Library / Konrad Wothe (tc); Nature Picture Library / Luiz Claudio Marigo (cla). Dreamstime.com: Cowboy54 (cra); Jocrebbin (tr); Feathercollector (cb); Afonso Farias (clb). 53 Alamy Stock Photo: FLPA (cb). Dreamstime.com: Agami Photo Agency (tl); Imogen Warren (tc); LImckinnie (tr); Rinus Baak (ca); Brian Kushner (bc); Simonas Minkevičius (b). Shutterstock.com: Agami Photo Agency (cla); MTKhaled mahmud (bl). 54 Dreamstime.com: Richard Lindie (bc); Graeme Snow (br). 54-55 Dreamstime.com: Designprintck (background). Getty Images: Stone / Rosemary Calvert. 55 Dreamstime.com: China Span / Keren Su (br). Getty Images / iStock: Carlos-B (tr). 56 Alamy Stock Photo: All Canada Photos / Roberta Olenick (bc). Dorling Kindersley: Gary Ombler (cr). Dreamstime.com: Rinus Baak (tl); Ian Dyball (tr); Ihor Smishko (sand background). 57 Dreamstime.com: Designprintck (background); Martin Pelanek (t); Mathilde Receveur (bl). naturepl.com: Michael Pitts (b). Shutterstock.com: Agami Photo Agency (c). 58 Alamy Stock Photo: Minden Pictures / Buiten-beeld / Otto Plantema (br). Dorling Kindersley: Stephen Oliver (clb, clb/pebbles). Dreamstime.com: Sue Feldberg (tr); Ihor Smishko (sand background); Ondřej Prosický (cl); Waldemar Knight (cl); Maciej Olszewski (bl). 58-59 Dreamstime.com: Ruslanchik / Ruslan Nassyrov (background). 59 Dreamstime.com: Steve Byland (tl); Imogen Warren (clb); Brian Lasenby (cr). Getty Images / iStock: Harry Collins (tc). 60 Dreamstime.com: Agami Photo Agency (br). naturepl.com: Hanne & Jens Eriksen (bl). 60-61 Dreamstime.com: Agami Photo Agency (c). 61 Alamy Stock Photo: Minden Pictures / BIA / Mathias Schaef (cb).

naturepl.com: Hanne & Jens Eriksen (cb). 62 123RF.com: agamiphoto (ca). Dreamstime.com: Dennis Jacobsen (bl). 63 Dreamstime.com: Agami Photo Agency (b); Henry Soesanto (cra); Charles Brutlag (cla). 64-65 Getty Images: Mint Images RF - Oliver Edwards. 65 Dreamstime.com: Designprintck (background); Michael Truchon (tr). 66 Dreamstime.com: Sergei Razvodovskij (background). 66-67 Dreamstime.com: Designprintck (background). 67 Dorling Kindersley: National Birds of Prey Centre, Gloucestershire (tr). 68 Alamy Stock Photo: All Canada Photos / Glenn Bartley (tr); Minden Pictures / BIA / Jan Wegener (tl). Dreamstime.com: Steve Byland (cr); Isselee (bl). 69 Alamy Stock Photo: All Canada Photos / Jared Hobbs (tl); Design Pics Inc / David Ponton (c); Dave Keightley (br). Getty Images / iStock: Angelika (r). 70 123RF.com: Thawat Tanhai (c). Dreamstime.com: Chamnan Phanthong (cra). 71 Dreamstime.com: Gentoomultimedia (cra); Yezhenliang (tc); Aris Triyono (br); (null) (null) (bc). 72 Dorling Kindersley: Natural History Museum, London (clb, cb). Dreamstime.com: Nfransua (cra); Elena Schweitzer (cra). 74 Dreamstime.com: Marcobarone (c); Stuartan (tl). 75 Dreamstime.com: Agami Photo Agency (c, cb); Michael Truchon (tl). 80 Dreamstime.com: Designprintck (background).

Cover images: *Front:* **Dorling Kindersley:** E.J. Peiker (tr); **Dreamstime.com:** Assoonas (kingfisher), Astrid228 / Astrid Gast (crb), Atman (t)/ (chestnut leaf x2), Svetlana Foote (jay), Jessamine (clb), Mikelane45 (bl); **Fotolia:** Eric Isselee (owl); **Getty Images / iStock:** PrinPrince (yellow bird). *Back:* **123RF.com:** Keith Levit (clb); **Dorling Kindersley:** Jerry Young (br); **Asherita Viajera:** (tl). *Spine:* **Dreamstime.com:** Astrid228 / Astrid Gast (t)/ (hinduracke).

All other images © Dorling Kindersley

For further information see: www.dkimages.com

ABOUT THE ILLUSTRATOR

Claire McElfatrick is a freelance artist. She created illustrated greetings cards before working on children's books. Claire has illustrated all the other books in this series: *The Magic and Mystery of Trees, The Book of Brilliant Bugs,* and *Earth's Incredible Oceans.*